A Gift for the Bereaved Parent

A remedy for grief from the Islamic perspective using quotes from the Qur'an and Hadith

Written and compiled by
Zamir Hussain

© BCH 2010
First Published in January 2010
Revised June 2023
by **Ta-Ha Publishers Ltd**
Unit 4, The Windsor Centre
Windsor Grove,
London, SE27 9NT, UK
Website: www.**tahapublishers.com**
E-mail: support@tahapublishers.com

Written and compiled by: **Zamir Hussain**
General Editor: **Dr. Abia Afsar-Siddiqui**
Design and layout by: **Shakir Abdulcadir**

A catalogue record of this book is available from the British Library
ISBN-13: 978 1 84200 284 1
Printed and bound by: **Imak Ofset, Türkiye**

Dedication
This book is dedicated to all those Muslim families we journey with in their grief.

Acknowledgements
We would like to thank Birmingham Children's Hospital Charities for the initial funding for this project, those who contributed to the consultation process and MidTECH - NHS Innovations West Midlands for their invaluable support in its production.

We would also like to thank Shakir Abdulcadir and the team at Open Squares creative design.

Red Balloon Resources
This booklet is a part of "Red Balloon Resources": Support in Multi-faith and Cultural Paediatric Health, Palliative and Bereavement Care. Further copies and information about other resources are available from the Project director, Paul Nash. All profits go towards the ongoing support of children, families and staff in Paediatric Health, Palliative and Bereavement Care.

بِسْمِ اللهِ الرَّحْمٰنِ الرَّحِيْمِ

Bismillahir Rahmanir Raheem
In the name of Allah, All-Merciful, Most Merciful

Surah al-Fatiha - The Opening

**Praise be to Allah, the Lord of all the worlds,
the All-Merciful, the Most Merciful, the King of the Day of Repayment.
You alone we worship. You alone we ask for help.
Guide us on the Straight Path, the path of those You have blessed,
not of those with anger on them, nor of the misguided.**
(Surah al-Fatiha, verses 1-7)

*The Prophet (peace be upon him) said:
'There is a cure for everything in the Opening of the Book.' [Surah al-Fatiha]
(Baihaqi and Darimi)*

Allah

I dedicate this book to my parents
and all those whose kindness
and support has paved my way.

Introduction

The loss of a child can bring immense anguish, sorrow and pain. Not only has the child gone, so too have the dreams and hopes of the future associated with the child. There can be secondary losses which may affect relationships, health and motivation. There can also be feelings of guilt or regret at what could have been said or done, as parents often have a strong sense of responsibility. A strong attachment and need to nurture the child may also remain.

Grieving is an important part of the healing process and people will grieve in different ways. Each experience is unique and individual, ranging from uncontrolled expression of despair to an inability to show emotion. However, usually there are initial disbelief and denial, then realisation that the loved one has actually died and acceptance of the spiritual journey of the deceased. There is also the adjusting to a new environment without the loved one and working through the grief and pain of separation.

It does not follow that these stages are reached systematically but one may alternate from one stage to another and take varying lengths of time. It is not unusual for the pain to always remain, increasing in intensity as some event or reminder renews the loss.

It is essential to know that people are susceptible to weakness and emotion. It is only natural that one sheds tears and has grief and sadness in the heart; this is valid and cannot be denied.

The Islamic perspective on bereavement requires a trust and belief in Allah [God] and His Messenger, the Prophet Muhammad (peace be upon him). Thus, the knowledge and remedy prescribed by the Qur'an (Word of Allah) and Hadith (words and actions of the Prophet, peace be upon him) have provided the same solace and guidance throughout the ages.

Islam guides to adopt *sabr* when faced with difficulty or calamity. *Sabr* is often translated as 'patience', but this is not adequate; literally *sabr* means courage, forbearance, perseverance, the acceptance of Allah's will and plan.

This book aims to provide knowledge and guidance in working towards *sabr* and understanding by using the Qur'an and Hadith. The design uses a soothing motif and Arabic calligraphy in the form of some of the ninety-nine Names [Attributes] of Allah. The Qur'an teaches the importance and benefits of calling upon Allah through His Names.

The book focuses on what a parent may experience during the struggle in coming to terms with the loss of a child. (*The parent's inner voice is written by the author, after listening to, and supporting bereaved parents in her role as a Muslim Chaplain. This will be seen in black italics.*)

However, this book can be useful to all who have been touched by bereavement and loss. For those facing difficulty, despair or other unresolved issues in life, be they sickness, emotional, material or spiritual. This book can also be beneficial in providing information for those wanting to know the Islamic perspective on the death of a child.

'O Compassionate and Most Merciful Lord! Send peace and blessings upon the Prophet Muhammad, through whose life and example we have come to know You and Your guidance. Give courage and strength to those who suffer grief and sorrow; for You are the Lord and Protector.' *Ameen.*

My prayer for you,
Zamir Hussain, *Muslim Chaplain,* January 2009, Birmingham UK.

Farewell my child

Oh my beautiful child! My love for you is eternal. I know that you are no longer with me. I cannot hold you or see you, yet I feel your presence, sometimes my eyes frantically search for you. I see you in the smile of a child, I hear your soft voice, and I smell your sweetness. I turn around expecting you to be there. How I hope that this has all been a bad dream, that I will wake up and find you in my arms smiling.

Your precious belongings are so dear to me. I embrace them to my heart and it feels as though I am connected to a part of you. I imagine how life would have been with you by my side. How I would have watched you grow and cherished you, laughed with you and wiped your tears.

Just as I feel this pain, this emptiness, this loneliness is too much to bear, I feel you saying, 'Please don't be sad. I will always be with you, this separation is brief. Soon I shall hold your hand and we will be together forever.'

We will test you
with a certain amount of fear and hunger
and loss of wealth and life and fruits.
But give good news to the steadfast:
Those who, when disaster strikes them, say,

'We belong to Allah
and to Him we will return.'

Those are the people
who will have blessings and mercy from their Lord;
they are the ones who are guided.

(Surah al-Baqarah, verses 155-157)

Muhammad sallallahu 'alaihi wa sallam
Muhammad, may the peace and blessings of Allah be upon him

The following letter of condolence was sent by the Prophet (peace be upon him) to Mu'adh ibn Jabal (may Allah be pleased with him) upon the death of Mu'adh's son.

In the name of Allah, All-Merciful, Most Merciful

May peace be with you. I praise Allah, there is no god but Allah. May Allah increase your reward and calm your sad heart and give you guidance and the power to thank Him. Indeed our lives, our families and our property are gifts entrusted to us only for a fixed time. The duty of a man is to thank Allah when He bestows on him a gift, and to endure with patience when He takes it back.

Your son was a special trust from Allah. He blessed you with him till He desired and took him away from you in return for a Great Reward. O Mua'dh, do not let complaining and impatience destroy your reward or you shall surely regret this later on. If you knew how much return and recompense has been granted to you for it, then you would be surely amazed at Allah's Mercy.

The promise which Allah has made to the people who endure misfortune and pain with patience shall be fully fulfilled in the life to come. The promise of Allah should reduce your grief. Whatever is destined to take place must occur.

May you be in peace.

Allah's Messenger Muhammad.

(Tabarani)

The Prophet (peace be upon him) said to his daughter Zainab (may Allah be pleased with her) as her child was dying:

'Whoever Allah takes is His and whatever He gives is His and to all things He has appointed a time so have patience and be rewarded.'
(Bukhari)

'What is this?' asked a Companion as the eyes of the Prophet (peace be upon him) started shedding tears and he replied:

'This is mercy which Allah has placed in the hearts of His servants. And indeed it is to only the merciful of His servants that Allah gives mercy.' (Bukhari)

O Allah, as I grieve for my child I think of how Your beloved Prophet Muhammad (peace be upon him) endured the loss and separation of those so dear to him. His parents, guardians, wife and children. And yet he did not falter in his mission. Please Lord, give me the ability to follow his great example.

The Prophet (peace be upon him) took his eighteen month old son Ibrahim, smelled him and kissed him. During Ibrahim's last breaths tears began to fall from the Prophet's (peace be upon him) eyes and he said: *'The eyes are shedding tears and the heart grieves. And we will not say except what pleases Allah.'* *(Bukhari)*

الصَّبُوْر

Al-Saboor
The Patient

الحَقُّ

Al-Haqq
The Truth

When a child of Allah's servant dies,

Allah says to His angels:

"Have you taken the life of My servant's child?"

They say, "Yes."

He says, "Have you taken the fruit of his heart?"

They say, "Yes."

He says, "What has My servant said?"

They say, "He has praised you and said,

'Indeed to Allah we belong and to Him is our return.'"

Allah says,

"Build a house for my servant in Paradise

and call it the House of Praise."

(Tirmidhi)

I will never forget my last gaze upon your angelic face, peaceful and radiant as if you were asleep. My darling you are free now, free from all pain and constraint.

My love for you is strong enough to let you go. Go to your heavenly home. You have touched our lives with a gentle glow of beauty that will always remain and a bond that no time or space can sever. You will always be in my heart.

It is reported that the deceased children will be in the blessed company of the Prophet Ibrahim (upon him be peace).

The Prophet (peace be upon him) reports a dream in which he saw a flourishing green garden with a huge tree. Near its root was sitting an old man with some children. He (peace be upon him) was told in his blessed dream that the old man was the Prophet Ibrahim (upon him be peace) and the children were the (deceased) offspring of the people. (Bukhari)

الْوَكِيْلُ

Al-Wakeel
The Trustee

الْوَدُود

Al-Wadood
The Loving

19

Their little ones are the
da'amis (helpers) of Paradise.
They will meet their parents
and grab them by their garments or their hands
to no end other than that
Allah will enter them into Paradise.
(Muslim)

By the One in whose hand is my soul,
the miscarried foetus will lead his mother to Paradise by his umbilical cord,
if she was patient, hoping to be rewarded.
(Ahmad)

And We will unite those who believed
with their offspring, who followed them in faith,
and We will not undervalue their own actions
in any way. Every man is in pledge
for what he earned.
(Surah al-Tur, verse 21)

Three days have passed since I said my last goodbye and the official period of mourning comes to a close. As some expectations of normality begin to set in, I feel a quiet panic. Must I face a new reality now? How can I live in a world without you?

The day had passed as if it had been a dream and I was watching it happening to someone else. Now I begin to feel the rawness, as if a limb had been torn from me. I busy myself afraid to stop and think. My mouth feels so dry that no amount of water seems to quench my thirst. I feel exhausted. I seem to be living with you, yet without you.

My mind urges me to forbearance, tells me that Allah is the Best of Planners. I am struggling. The inner battle for calm goes on, yet I put on a brave face.

O Allah, I pray for strength. Your Love and Mercy for me is greater than mine for my child. I know You will not leave me helpless. You will be with me even as I lie awake in the darkness of the night. I place my trust in You Lord, for indeed You are the Writer of Destinies:

Say: 'Nothing can happen to us except what Allah has ordained for us. He is our Master. It is in Allah that the believers should put their trust.'

(Surah al-Tawbah, verse 51)

Know that if the people gathered together to benefit you with something, they could not benefit you unless Allah had written it down for you and if they gathered to harm you with something, they could not do so unless Allah had written it down for you. The pens have been raised and the scrolls have dried.

(Tirmidhi)

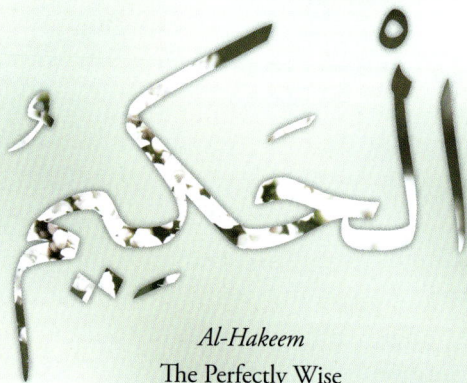

Al-Hakeem
The Perfectly Wise

O Allah, I know that everything happens for a reason, even so there are so many questions that fog my mind. Please help me to understand why this has happened to me.

Or did you suppose that you would enter the Garden without facing the same as those who came before you...
(Surah al-Baqarah, verse 214)

The most afflicted among the people are the Prophets, then the best, then the next and so on. A person is afflicted according to his rank. If his faith is firm his trials are intense and if his faith is weak his trials are light. Indeed, a servant of Allah continues to be subjected to adversities until he walks upon the earth free of all sins. (Bukhari)

No fatigue nor disease nor sorrow nor sadness,
nor hurt nor distress befall a Muslim
even if it was a prick of a thorn but Allah removes some of his sin.
(Bukhari)

Strange are the ways of a believer,
for there is good in his every affair.
For if he has occasion to feel delight he thanks Allah
and at times of adversity
he shows resignation and endures patiently.
There is good for him.
(Muslim)

I try to understand my Lord, yet feel bowed down by grief. I take refuge in the knowledge that even Your beloved Prophets cried out to You at times of difficulty.

Prophet Ya'qub (upon him be peace) at the separation from his son Yusuf (upon him be peace) said: **'What anguish is my sorrow for Yusuf!' And then his eyes turned white from hidden grief. They said, 'By Allah, you will not ever cease to mention Yusuf, till you waste away or are among the people of the grave!' He said, 'I make complaint about my grief and sorrow to Allah alone.'** *(Surah Yusuf, verses 84-86)*

And Prophet Nuh (upon him be peace) cried out to his Lord: **'I am overwhelmed, so help me!'** *(Surah al-Qamar, verse 10)*

Misfortune and hardship afflicted them
and they were shaken to the point that
the Messenger and those who believed with him said,
'When is Allah's help coming?'
Be assured that Allah's help is very near.

(Surah al-Baqarah, verse 214)

Indeed Lord, You do not leave me helpless. Your Mercy descends in so many ways.
You sent down Your Word [the Qur'an].
I ask You, O Allah, make the Qur'an a source of release for my anxieties,
and a delight and light of my heart.

We send down in the Qur'an
that which is a healing and mercy to the believers.

(Surah Bani Isra'il, verse 82)

You sent your beloved Prophet Muhammad (peace be upon him) as a mercy to all people. Through his blessed person the knowledge of Your boundless Love and Compassion are shown to us, and to us is demonstrated a perfect example. O Allah, accept my feeble effort and lift the burden from my being.

Allah showed great kindness to the believers when He sent a Messenger to them from among themselves to recite His Signs to them and purify them and teach them the Book and Wisdom.
(Surah Ali Imran, verse 164)

You have an excellent model in the Messenger of Allah, for all who put their hope in Allah and the Last Day and remember Allah much.
(Surah al-Ahzab, verse 21)

Allah and His angels call down blessings on the Prophet. You who believe! Call down blessings on him and ask for complete peace and safety for him.
(Surah al-Ahzab, verse 56)

27

الرَّؤُوفُ

Al-Rauf
The Compassionate

O Allah, You comforted Your beloved Prophet (peace be upon him), assuring him of Your Presence, as he faced difficulty after difficulty, and felt the crushing burden of his mission. You gave him courage and hope, directing him to turn to You with dedication and effort. And You promise all believers when You say:

Have you taken a promise from Allah? For Allah never breaks His Promise. *(Surah al-Baqarah, verse 80)*

For truly with hardship comes ease; truly with hardship comes ease. So when you have finished, work on, and make your Lord your goal! *(Surah al-Inshirah, verses 5-8)*

My Allah, You send me strength in my own being,
promising that this pain is not beyond what I can bear.
I know that I am free to choose a path.
O Allah, help me to chose a path wherein I can grow and gain
in wisdom and strength
and make easy for me resolve and courage.

On no soul
does Allah place a burden
greater than it can bear.
(Surah al-Baqarah, verse 286)

Through Your Compassion Lord, You send your angels. Is it Your angels, Lord? My heart hears whispering words of comfort.

Standing over you are guardians, noble, recording.
(Surah al-Infitar, verses 10-11)

Everyone has a succession of angels in front of him and behind him, guarding him by Allah's command.
(Surah al-Ra'd, verse 11)

[The angels say] We are your protectors in the life of this world and the Next World. You will have there all that your selves could wish for.
(Surah Fussilat, verse 31)

الْوَلِيُّ

Al-Waliyy
The Protecting Friend

الرَّحِيم

Al-Raheem
The Most Merciful

Allah, You sent the gift of Salah [ritual prayer] and as I prepare,
the cool water of ablution soothes as it washes over me.
I look forward to this sacred time and space when everything else is put on hold.
I lay my heart bare, and my soul finds solace in being alone with You.
In prostration I feel closest to You.

You who believe!
Seek help in steadfastness and the prayer.
(Surah al-Baqarah, verse 153)

You sent, O Allah, the power of Du'a [supplication]
the most sincerest of Worship and connection to You.
I know You hear my every sigh, my every call as I turn to You in Du'a.
Grant me from Your Wisdom Lord, even that which I do not know to ask.

If My slaves ask you about Me, I am near.
I answer the call of the caller when he calls on Me.
They should therefore respond to Me and believe in Me
so that hopefully they will be rightly guided.
(Surah al-Baqarah, verse 186)

O Allah, indeed ultimately You are the greatest gift of gifts, the greatest treasure.

Only in the remembrance of Allah can the heart find peace.
(Surah al-Ra'd, verse 28)

My Lord, at times I cannot find the words to call out to You,
then I feel Your Love take my outstretched hand as it yearns to be held by You;
and You comfort me in my silence.
Yet You gift me with the perfect words when I have need of words.

When distressed or in sorrow the Prophet (peace be upon him) would say:

يَا حَيُّ يَا قَيُّوْمُ بِرَحْمَتِكَ اَسْتَغِيْثُ

Ya hayyu ya qayyum, bi rahmatika astaghithu
O the Living, O the Eternal, I seek help in Your Grace.
(Tirmidhi)

To Allah belong the Most Beautiful Names, so call on Him by them.

(Surah al-A'raf, verse 180)

يَا صَبُوْرُ

Ya Saboor
O Giver of Forbearance,
grant me *sabr*.

يَا سَلَامُ

Ya Salaam
O Giver of Peace,
grant me Peace.

يَا لَطِيْفُ

Ya Lateef
O the Subtle the Aware,
I release my plight to You.

لَا حَوْلَ وَ لَا قُوَّةَ اِلَّا بِاللهِ

La hawla wa la quwwata illa billah.
There is neither power nor strength except through Allah.

الْمُجِيبُ

Al-Mujeeb
The Responder to Prayer

O Allah, grant me:

Ihtisab: belief without doubt that You, O Lord, will compensate and reward for any discomfort no matter how large or small.

Istirja: knowing that only You are the Creator and Sustainer. Everything belongs to You and is a trust from You.

Rida: awareness of the peak of spiritual status to be content with Allah's Will and Wisdom in all circumstances.

O Allah, bless me with a beautiful patience and bring a stillness and serenity to my heart, and to the hearts of those whose love and care surround me and to those who also share this grief.

Allah, You send the magnificent gift of sabr. This is a time of a great test of sabr for me. Indeed how can the rewards of this gift be attained without hardships. I know You test those You love the most, bringing them closer and closer. O Allah, make me worthy of Your Love. Grant me resilience, fortitude and understanding.

The example of a believer is that of a fresh tender plant.
From whatever direction the wind comes it bends accordingly,
but when the wind becomes quiet it becomes straight again.
Similar is a believer when struck with a calamity.
(Bukhari)

I have no better reward than Paradise for a believing servant of Mine
who is patient and resigned when I take away one of his beloved,
one he cherished most in this world.
(Bukhari)

They will say, 'Praise be to Allah Who has removed all sadness from us.
Truly our Lord is Ever-Forgiving, Ever-Thankful:
He Who has lodged us, out of His munificence, in the Abode of Permanence
where no weariness or fatigue affects us.'
(Surah Fatir, verses 34-35)

الْغَفُور

Al-Ghafoor
The Forgiver

التَّوَّابُ

Al-Tawwab
The Acceptor of Repentance

الْعَفُوُّ

Al-Afuww
The Pardoner

The closest of the doors to You, O Allah, is the door of Shukr [gratitude].
Make me of the grateful and give me the endurance to thank You at every turn.
If the seas were ink they would run dry
and the words of Your Grace and blessings not yet written.
Amongst these gifts Lord, are the precious memories of my child
and the promise of love and joy that awaits.

Whoever gives thanks only does so to his own gain.
Whoever is ungrateful, my Lord is Rich Beyond Need, Generous.
(Surah al-Naml, verse 40)

If you are grateful, I will certainly give you increase.
(Surah Ibrahim, verse 7)

Everyone in the heavens and earth requests His aid.
Every day He is engaged in some affair.
So which of your Lord's blessings do you both then deny?
(Surah al-Rahman, verse 29-30)

الشَّكُورُ

Al-Shakoor
The Appreciative

Al-Kareem
The Generous

O Allah,

please help me to expect only the best from you.

I know that Your Mercy and Forgiveness are greater than my weakness.

Please pardon me when I falter, do not leave me to myself even for a moment.

Restore me Lord, and make me whole for You are the Guardian, the Benefactor.

I am as My servant thinks I am.

I am with him when he makes mention of Me.

If he makes mention of Me to himself, I make mention of him to Myself

and if he makes mention of Me in an assembly,

I make mention of him in an assembly better than it.

And if he draws near to Me an arm's length,

I draw near to him a fathom's length.

And if he comes to Me walking, I go to him at speed.

(Hadith Qudsi: Bukhari)

O Allah,
make me a source of mercy to others,
ease for me my sorrow in the remembrance of those who also suffer.
Open my heart to the plight of others.

Whoever makes things easy for others in this world, Allah will make
things easy for him both in this world and in the Hereafter…
Allah helps His servant as long as
His servant is engaged in helping his brother.
(Muslim)

Those who give away their wealth by night and day,
secretly and openly, will have their reward with their Lord.
They will feel no fear and they will know no sorrow.
(Surah al-Baqarah, verse 274)

الْهَادِي

Al-Hadi
The Guide

*These days seem to pass so slowly and
each moment weighs heavy. However, I
know that this will not last forever. With
Your help Lord, the shadows will lift
and sadness will ease. How the joys and
sorrows of the past have made me what I
am today, yet it all seems like it has been
a dream that lasted but a few moments.
Indeed You say that life in this world
will seem so brief. Help me Lord, to see
what is important, to walk in gentleness
and peace, submitting myself to You.*

**By the Late Afternoon, truly man
is in loss – except for those who
believe and do right actions and
urge each other to the truth and
urge each other to steadfastness.**
(Surah al-'Asr)

**On the Day they see it, it will
be as if they had only lingered for
the evening or the morning of
a single day.**
(Surah al-Naziat, verse 46)

The Dunya [worldly life] as compared to the Akhirah [the Hereafter]
is just like when one of you dips his finger in the sea.
Let him see how much water his finger will carry.
(al-Jami)

الْمُؤْمِنُ

Al-Mu'min
The Guardian of Faith

My Lord, I know my child was a trust from You.
What a great and eternal blessing You gave me.

With the passing of time perhaps I will grow stronger and wiser.

As the dawn rises after a dark night and the sun's warmth melts the winter frosts.

As a rainbow bejewels a grey sky and birdsong drifts in upon a gentle breeze.

As the spring brings forth colour and beauty,
And blossoms sweetly scent the air.

And I see others who travel with loss,
Smiling, once more.

I have hope and I trust in You, My Lord.

O Allah, illuminate my heart and cast light on my tongue,
light in my eye, light in my ears, light on my right, light on my left,
light above me, light before me, light behind me and
radiate my soul and give me immense light.
(Muslim)

الُنّوُر

Al-Noor
The Light

Oh my beautiful child! You are now
in the realms of Wisdom and Truth,
cherished and content,
you see what I do not see,
you know that which I do not know.
My soul hears your whispers of
comfort and peace,
embracing and healing,
breaking through the barriers
of space and time.
Death cannot end our bond of love.
One day the veils will lift,
the separation will cease,
and we will be together forever.

Peace until we meet again.

السَّلَامُ

Al-Salaam

The Source of Peace

إِنَّا لِلَّهِ وَإِنَّا إِلَيْهِ رَاجِعُونَ

Inna lillah wa inna ilayhi raji'un
To Allah we belong and to Him we return

Further support

Further support is available
from the following child bereavement support organisations.

www.childbereavementuk.org

www.childhoodbereavementnetwork.org.uk

www.childdeathhelpline.org.uk

www.winstonswish.org.uk

www.sands.org.uk

www.cruse.org.uk

You may also find a local organisation to you through your local hospital.
Please contact these organisations for additional support for family and friends.
They have leaflets, remembrance and support ideas,
web based forums, telephone help lines etc.